Finding God in crisis.

Bible studies that strengthen faith.

Pastor Gonzalo Sanabria.

<u>**Books by Pastor Gonzalo Sanabria**</u>.

DEDICATION

I dedicate this book to my good God, for his love and patience with me. To Jesus Christ my Savior and master and the Holy Spirit blessed comforter. To my beautiful wife Andrea gift of God and my son Daniel.

THANKS

To my family, to the Church that God allows me to graze (for their support and prayers), to all those who read our publications, and of course God who gives me the strength and the ability to write and develop the ministry that he has made me.

Contents

INTRODUCTION

It is very important to become aware of this truth: crises are part of the way. One day they come into our life or family and without warning they simply show up. We realize that it is inevitable, and we must deal with them.

Some are mild and disappear quickly, but others are more durable and generate great pressure. What to do in these situations?

Sometimes the day is very beautiful and suddenly the sky turns gray, the rain appears, then there are strong winds and storms that cause a lot of damage. Sometimes our life is going through a good time and suddenly everything turns gray and very difficult, the problems multiply and we do not know exactly how to act.

From the Christian perspective, this book exposes the reality of crises, their diversity, their impact on our humanity, the various reactions, and of course the Christian principles to face and overcome these circumstances.

From the Bible, we expose the various ways and attitudes of patriarchs, prophets, apostles, and various people in the face of the most adverse situations and how their faith in God led them to great victories.

Pastor Gonzalo Sanabria Anzola.

It is very important to become aware of this truth: crises are part of the way. One day they come into our life or family and without warning they simply show up. We realize that it is inevitable, we must deal with them. Sometimes they are the results of our bad decisions or for not having acted on time.

In the face of crisis or difficulty, we can react in very different ways. Some are victims of intense anger (causing more damage or pain), others whose hearts are flooded by pain only cry inconsolably, some others flee from the scene or situation (thus trying to evade reality), among others.

All these reactions do not address the situations as such, surely as human beings at first we act like this, but it is necessary to calm the heart and reflect before reacting.

We can easily fall prey to anxiety and anxiety and make hasty decisions putting at risk not only our life and future but that of our entire family. Anguish can lead us to do crazy things, and stress not only robs us of sleep, but it even affects our immune system which makes us vulnerable to disease.

Let us consider the case of a woman named Hagar, who in the face of the crisis fled, but in the midst of all this situation, she obtains great lessons.

This woman (Hagar) faces a very hard and difficult stage in her life, her wife Sarai afflicts her and despises her, she then decides to flee (as we sometimes do or think about adversity, but we must consider the example of Jesus who does not he fled, but went on in the power of the Spirit of God and trusting in divined protection).

"And because Sarai grieved her, she fled from her presence. And she was found by the angel of God by a source of water in the desert, by the source that is on the way to Shur. And she said to him: Hagar, Sarai's maid, where do you come from, and where are you going?

And she answered: I flee from Sarai, my lady. And she said to him the angel of God: Return to your mistress and be submissive under her hand" Genesis 16:6-9b.

The Angel of Jehovah is God himself, says the text that found her "in the desert", she fled to the desert, we see God searching, locating, following his children in the midst of crises, in the midst of difficulties.

Sometimes the son of God goes to the desert at the direction of the Lord (for example, Jesus "went to the desert led by the Spirit"), but other times we are the ones who get there, how it happened with Hagar (a desert is a difficult place for life, with extreme scarcity, a place of loneliness and many adversities).

"The way of Shur" is a significant location, since Shur means wall, rough wall, wall, and it lets us see those times when we "walk" but do not advance, it is stagnation, although full of activities. This happens because by moving away from God's will we become sterile, without fruit.

The goodness of God.

The Angel of the Lord asks Hagar about her situation and her plan to follow. Hagar has a great privilege here, she is visited by God (Hagar means foreigner, she was not from God's people, but the Lord was aware of her), who expresses her desire to listen to her, to know how she was.

God was interested in his difficulty and even in knowing what he was thinking of doing, and I think that Hagar, like us, expected a response from the Angel where it was justified and why not, perhaps a reprimand for Sarai for the Sarai for her way of acting.

God does not always do or respond as we want or expect. For the Lord responds to Hagar: "Turn to your mistress and be submissive under her hand", a response that surprises Hagar.

Let us remember that Hosea 2:14 "But behold, I will draw her and take her to the desert, and I will speak of her to hers in her heart". Sometimes God tells us what we do not want to hear, but the Lord knows what he does in us and others, and he does everything motivated by his love, we just have to obey.

Faced with crises, the first thing we must do is seek the presence of God to receive direction, and not make mistakes and go down the path of pain, or stagnate before our own pride.

God wants to lead us to his will for our blessing and honoring his Name. The fundamental principles to face and overcome the crisis are in detail later.

(I invite you to read the book of sermons by the same author: Sermon Outlines on the Whole Bible).

Chapter 2: THERE IS A GREAT OPPORTUNITY BEHIND EVERY PROBLEM.

Sometimes the day is very beautiful and suddenly the sky turns gray, the rain appears, and there are still strong winds and storms that cause a lot of damage. Sometimes our life is going through a good time and suddenly everything turns gray and very difficult, the problems multiply and we do not know exactly what to do.

But when we approach God, he shines with his glory, and everything is transformed by the power and care that he has for his children.

However, we ask ourselves why do we sometimes live in such difficult times? Perhaps because we have trusted more in our judgment, than in the wisdom of God. We often decide what to do without consulting the Lord.

At other times we do the opposite of what we know God has said, and of course, the results are painful, many times the storms of life have their origin in this attitude: our self-pride.

At other times we trust more in our abilities than in God's favor. Acts 27:9-11 tells us:

"Paul admonished them, saying: Men, I see that the navigation is going to be with damage and much loss, not only of the cargo and the ship but also of our people. But the centurion gave more credit to the pilot and the skipper of the ship, than to what Paul said".

We see that what the apostle said came from God, but they were more confident in their experience as sailors. They thought that with their abilities they could not only overcome the whole situation but that a storm was impossible since they did not see anything in particular. God always sees beyond what our eyes see.

At other times it may be because God wants to lead us to new levels of maturity. We speak of new levels of faith or responsibility, or perhaps God wants to teach us a greater dependence on him, or perhaps we must acknowledge our inabilities, or the Lord wants to show us how proud we are, etc. Behind every crisis, there is a great opportunity for growth and maturation.

What is the time when the problems appear and why?

It is a very interesting question, and I wish we had a precise and clear answer. But we can see several moments and reasons, for example: when based on the experience we mistakenly conclude that it is the time to act, it happened to Paul and the sailors who were taking him to Rome: Acts 27:13-14

"And blowing a breeze from the south, seeming to them that they already had what they wanted, they weighed anchor and sailed along the coast of Crete. But not long after, a hurricane wind called Euroclydon hit the ship".

They concluded that it was time to start the journey, but shortly after Euroclidon: a hurricane wind hit the ship. This shows us that it came unexpectedly and hit the ship with great force, so much so that it seemed to be sinking. They were sailors, experts, and connoisseurs of wind currents and the sea, but it was not enough. We must depend on God.

Problems also come when we settle into our comforts, neglecting the Lord's plan. We see this for example in the persecution that God allowed against the Jerusalem church in the first century of the Christian era.

For having received the command to go through the nations, and having been filled with the Holy Spirit, they stayed in the capital city of Israel. So crises also help us wake up to the passivity we can fall into.

Difficulties are opportunities to see the glory of God.

We see this throughout Scripture. Paul and the sailors saved by the hand of God reached their destination having overcome various difficulties during the journey. God protected them supernaturally and in the same way before problems, we must trust in the power of the Lord because he will us and advise us to get ahead.

Let's remember for example when Moses was eighty years old and shepherded in the desert, God called him to liberate the people from him and break the power of the Egyptian empire. When Abraham thought his son Isaac was going to die on Mount Moriah, God sent the provision.

When the Israelites thought they were going to die because they had the Red Sea ahead and Pharaoh was coming with his army behind, God opened the sea.

When they believed that they would die of thirst in the desert, God drew water from the rock. Every crisis we must see as an opportunity to see the glory of God.

God is almighty, nothing takes you by surprise. No matter how big the storm is, if we trust God we will see the power and glory of him in all circumstances of life. Behind every crisis, there is a great opportunity. God is bigger than any problem.

What does the apostle Paul do in the face of the storm?

Acts 27:15-20, lets us see several things that happened as a result of the storm that hit them at sea: they lost the ability to drive (there is no human control), with fear they reinforced the ship (there are fears) before the Raging storm began to settle, this means that they began to throw the load overboard (they had losses), there is no sun or stars for many days (the sailors used them to locate and navigate, this is a symbol of when time passes and no you see a response from heaven) and finally, hope is a lot.

Despite adversity, it is necessary to strengthen faith in God and maintain hope in him. We do this by strengthening intimacy with God. We also see that Paul was able to give them a word of encouragement, and assurance because he had been in the presence of God.

In the face of adversity, we must give more value to "us" than to "I and you" (Acts 27:33-36). Pablo was the prisoner that these sailors were taking to Rome, however, his attitude was not one of revenge, he was interested in the welfare of others, his attitude and good spirits caused positive changes in them.

Pablo was aware that they were all on the same ship, it is not a question of who arrives first, but that we must all arrive. Acts 27:44.

God has promised to be with us every day, surely some days are more difficult than others but we must face them trusting in God, seeking his presence, aware that the Lord has power over all storms.

After the storm, they arrived on the island of Malta, and there many were healed and had the testimony of Jesus Christ (Acts 28). So after the storm comes not only calm but great victories and conquests.

Chapter 3: IT IS POSSIBLE TO OVERCOME THE FAMILY CRISIS

The marriage of Joseph and Mary was designed from heaven, they were blameless, and they loved God, and were faithful in everything. In his home, the Savior of the world would be born and raised.

Despite all this, they had difficulties and crises to overcome, for example when Mary appeared pregnant by the Holy Spirit, Joseph thought about secretly abandoning her (and thus not exposing her to punishment for infidelity). But the Lord revealed to Joseph that this was a supernatural work of God.

We see in this case how God takes care of families. Consider Matthew 2:13-14 "Then… an angel of the Lord appeared in a dream to Joseph and said: Get up and take the child and his mother, and flee to Egypt, and stay there until I tell you; because it will come to pass that Herod will look for the child to kill him. And he, waking up, took the child and his mother at night, and went to Egypt".

God sent an angel to warn Mary's husband. Joseph is the figure of the priest in the house. Joseph represents the man in the house. Joseph represents the man in the home.

He had a dream where the Lord told him where to go, and he should depend on God to know when to return the Lord also reveals the danger to him: Herod God does not change, and he desires to reveal His plans to His children and to warn of the dangers of the way.

Joseph was in Egypt until Herod died (Matthew 2:15). Imagine if he came back sooner, he would have exposed his entire family to danger. We can expose our family in many ways:

Regarding children: permissiveness of friends that incite them to drugs and the wrong things. Absence of love and incorrect discipline, internet and TV without regulation and instruction, etc.

Regarding the spouse: due to the absence of communication, financial irresponsibility, absence of intimate life, excess of work and commitments, etc.

Projects that involve the future of the family without consulting God (business, loans, travel or extended absences, etc).

We expose the family by abandoning fellowship with God, by allowing bitterness to rule the heart, and by not providing for the home.

The Bible also teaches us that all this was to fulfill what was written (then Joseph represents a man who advances guided by the Word of God). It is therefore very important to avoid falling into crisis or painful consequences to fill our heart with the Word of God, as it will be for us "a lamp on the path and a light for our feet".

Let's take care of our children.

God's enemy seeks toy destroy children (Matthew 2:16-18). In this biblical passage we must highlight several words or phrases that leave us with several important teachings, for example:

The name Herod means the dragon of fire. Revelation twelve teaches us that the dragon will chase the woman's son (where the woman represents Israel and the son represents the seed of the Jews).

The text tells us: "He got very angry, and ordered all the children to be killed". We see what provokes anger. Hasty decisions, foolish orders, anger can lead to murder, for example, Cain killed his brother Abel.

The "Children of Bethlehem" are a symbol of the purposes and plans that God has with each one of us; Bethlehem means: "House of bread" but unfortunately that generation was destroyed by the enemy.

It is very important to see that this story teaches us the role of the man who ensures family security (Matthew 2:19-21). Let us remember that the Bible teaches that the man is the head, which that speaks to us of government, of authority and power to cover.

God made Eve from a man's rib, close to her heart to be loved and under her arm to be protected. She needs an atmosphere of security, and man is charge of generating it (of course with the wisdom and support of God).

José is warned by the Lord through dreams, he is a man of communion with God, who allows and accepts divine guidance. The Bible also tells us that "he took the child and his mother" this shows us that he was busy seeking the welfare of his family.

He is thinking of this wife and his son (some do not care about his spouse or his children, and even less do they think about a stable future).

Joseph made decisions guided by God, he was not driven by this emotions, nor because they told him to go to this place because he is good, he received divine direction: Matthew 2:22-23.

Now there are no longer two, but only one, work is also as a team, because we are a complement. We see in Mary a wise and prudent woman who respects her husband and who surely supported him in prayer.

Dialogue is a fundamental column in the home. When communication breaks down or neglects in the When communication breaks down or neglects in the married couple, it is only a matter of time before everything begins to collapse, the same happens with the children.

When the couple communicates, cultivates dialogue, and does the same with their children, we speak of a solid family, which together will withstand the strong winds of the storms that come against the house.

Marriage is a design from heaven, it is a not human invention, God wants children to have a stable home, as parents we are challenged to seek the Lord's direction and not make hasty decisions that put our family at risk. God wants the best for us and our children.

If the crisis has touched the doors of our house, like Joseph we must seek God in intimacy, seek his wisdom and diligently act from him, because God is with us and we will see the glory of him over the family crisis. We will study in detail later a complete chapter on the principles to face and overcome crises.

Chapter 4: THE RESTORATION OF A FAMILY AFFECTED BY A CRISIS

Families go through various stages, some good and happy, others not so good and rather sad. Sometimes the marriage breaks down, the children stray from the right path, financial ruin comes, or a serious illness, etc. However, in all these cases God must be our guide, strength, and source of wisdom.

The Bible tells us the story of a widow who lost her only child. Without a doubt, it is a great crisis. It is interesting to see that in this difficult scenario Jesus appeared and many were following him:

"It happened later, that he was going to the city called Nain, and many of his disciples were going with him, and a great multitude", Luke 7:11.

The crowds followed Jesus for various reasons: They recognized him as the Messiah, for his power to perform miracles, for the miracles of provision he did (for example the multiplication of the fishes and the loaves), for his restorative power (they came paralyzed, lepers, demonized, etc).

What the Bible clearly teaches us is that apart from God we can do nothing, without him everything is more difficult. Peter told him: "Lord, where else will we go, if only you have the words of eternal life", that is why we must follow Jesus, he is the way, the truth, and the life, without him the human being experiences the emptiness of his heart and a great confusion without clear meaning in his life.

Sometimes adverse and difficult situations get worse (Luke 7:12). The widow's son is dead. The deceased was "his mother's only child" was a young man and surely supported the home; her mother was a widow, in the Sacred Scriptures the term widow generally refers to a woman who, having lost her husband, has been left destitute, with severe difficulties supporting her. Losing her husband had already been very hard, but now she also loses her son.

Sometimes the crisis or difficulty at home worsens, but God is faithful and does not abandon his children. Let us remember that when the widow of Sarepta of Sidon was going through the drought and thought that she was already going to die with her son, God sent her provision through Elijah. Although the test is difficult, God does not abandon his people, he takes care of his children.

It is vital to trust in the goodness of God: "And when the Lord saw her, he had compassion on her, and said: Do not cry", Luke 7:13. Here we see the love of Jesus for humanity (for that love he gave her life for our salvation), he felt sorry for her, Jesus was not indifferent to her sadness and pain, as sometimes the enemy wants us to think.

The biblical text also tells us that Jesus told her: "do not cry", he consoled her, remember that the Scriptures tell us: "Blessed be the God and Father of our Lord Jesus Christ... who comforts us in all our tribulations", also Scripture tells us that the Holy Spirit is our comforter, then the Son comforts, the Father comforts and the Holy Spirit also, all three comfort the believer, because God knows that even though we are His children sometimes we go through the tribulation, and we need His help and strength.

Jesus knows how to do things.

We can trust God, he knows what it is to be tempted, Jesus lived it, he knows what it is to be tired, he knows that it is a betrayal, he knows that it is loneliness and misunderstanding, that is why such a high priest suited us, Jesus Christ, one in whom we can deposit all our heart, he will not fail us. In this home there was a crisis, Jesus appeared at the right time and continues to do the same today.

Talk to God and put your heart in him. Faith trusts in the omnipotence of the Lord. Luke 7:14 tells us about the actions of Jesus, and we can see several very important things:

"He touched the coffin": the Law prevented this because it caused ritual impurity, less in his capacity as Master of the Law. But, he did it to show that he has power over all things, even over death (there is no crisis too great for God).

"And He said": here we must highlight the power of His word, in all the miracles of the gospels that Jesus did, the word was always present because the Word of God is full of power, which is why the Lord says: "The word that it comes out of my mouth and it will fulfill what it is sent for".

"Get up": the young man had died, everything was over, but there was Jesus and that is the most important thing. Jesus has the power to restore what has been lost (v. 15).

God's work in our midst should produce our praise, fear of God in our hearts, and recognition of his power and love (v. 16-17).

We see that in this family a deep crisis came, that day when Jesus arrived everyone was crying, the mother of this young man was left alone and without someone to support her, the future was dark, but there Jesus appeared with his power and everything was transformed.

Faith sees beyond circumstances; sets his eyes on the goal and does not stop in adversity; see the greatness of God even if the problems are large. Faith trust in the power of the Lord even though time passes and for mean it becomes late.

Faith places its whole being in the promises of the One who does not lie. A person of faith is one whose heart is aware that even though there are adversities, God will show his glory in the end and we will have obtained great teachings.

Crises do not distinguish between people. The Bible teaches us that Jesus had a special love for the Lazarus family, John 11:5. It was the family that hosted him when he was passing through to Jerusalem.

There Mary anointed him with perfume, John 11:2. When Jesus arrived, Lazarus has died (Jesus love him), so we see that his love does not mean the absence of crisis, but victory over the crisis.

In a crisis, God shows his glory, John 11:1, 3-4. The Bible does not tell us what Lazarus disease was. This moment was difficult, not only because he was a loved one, but because he worked to support the house, he was the man who represented the sisters, the future looked dark and complicated… but Jesus expresses that in this situation the Glory of God.

In the face of pressure and the crisis itself, we may be driven to act madly, but we must calm our hearts to make wise decisions. God does things in his time, John 11:6-7.

When he told the Lord that Lazarus had died, he did not rush out to Bethany. Jesus was on the banks of the Jordan River, and he would arrive at the right time to glorify the heavenly Father. God does not delay or anticipate, he arrives at the right time.

Crisis are opportunities to know God more.

Marta knew about the resurrection, but she did not know who the resurrection, but she did not know who the resurrection and the life were, John 11:20-27. Martha as a good Jewess was taught about the resurrection on the last day. But all this knowledge falls before the revelation of Jesus.

The Lord Jesus is the giver of life, and that power is above death itself, we will also see it in the rapture of the church. Jesus reveals himself as the one who is the resurrection and the life, this was something completely new for Martha.

Jesus knows and knows what you live and feel, John 11:32-35. Here we see an expressions of the humanity of Jesus. The Bible tells us: "Jesus wept" shaken in his spirit and moved. Scripture shows us Jesus crying here, crying in Gethsemane, he wept for Jerusalem (Luke 19:41).

Jesus is no stranger to our difficulties and crises, he understands and strengthens us so that we can move on. The reality is that although sometimes we doubt it, Jesus is with us and he knows our struggles, crises, and mistakes, also what we fell and live in the midst of them.

The Lord Jesus has power over all things, John 11:38-40. The miracle was more difficult (humanly) because: the cave had a stone placed on it. Lazarus was already stinking since he dead been four days old.

For Marta and Maria, the miracle was no longer possible. For everyone there was nothing to do, just cry, John 11:18-19, 31. Furthermore, death already had Lazarus in his hands.

Our trust in God must be above negative voices, adversity, our feelings of failure, and rather we must go to the presence of him.

Jesus prayed and declared the word of life, and Lazarus was resurrected. He came out of the grave. This reminds and teaches us that in the midst of crisis God strengthens us, teaches us, and help us overcome the various obstacles in life.

We all face problems or crisis. When we look at the Bible we see that no one was exempt from them. Even our own Lord Jesus was rejected, slandered, betrayed, etc. The Bible also teaches us that trials will come and that they help us grow. The point is that we all act in different ways before them.

Sometimes the results of our plans, projects, and work produce anguish and bitterness, in David's life it happened: his sons and for his daughters, 1 Samuel 30:6.

David, from the persecution of King Saul, had hidden among the Philistines and was posing as an Israelite faithful to them. When he returns to the land he finds everything destroyed and the women had been taken with his children: 1 Samuel 30:1-4. Sometimes extremely painful and frustrating moments come into our lives.

The hearts of the people who followed David had been filled with bitterness, so much so that they thought of stoning him. Sadness, anger, and disappointment can lead humans to do crazy things.

Sometimes in the face of crisis, the leaderships we exorcises is undervalued. The Bible teaches us that the people who spoke of stoning David, these stones would be loaded with anger, resentment, anger, we see then how an angry feeling can kill a great affection.

We can think of the exercise of leadership in the family, in the company, university, church, or any group, and experience contempt in the face of the crisis, because by leading many they conclude that the difficulty is due to bad leadership. We must be aware that this can happen.

Let's avoid the wrong attitudes in the face of the crisis. Before her we can complain, annoy us, murmur, plead, get angry with others, abandon everything, and blame others for what happened, or express many excuses to justify ourselves.

Those who followed David became angry and project their anger against him and the way to get that anger out is by throwing stones at him.

How did David react to the crisis? Let's observe his behavior in this situation (1 Samuel 30:6b-8). The Bible tells us that he sought God and was strengthened in him. He consulted the Lord to know what he was to do.

He made sure of the Lord's backing. So let's not do things foolishly, as this can cause loss, wear, pain, and greater embarrassment.

Always keep in mind that you are an example to others. Critical or high-pressure situations (like the one that happened to David) allow us to see our true character.

All those who followed David had the opportunity to see the face and actions of his leader in the face of such a situation: the pain of loss, and the threats from his own men. David's behavior in such a situation marked the hearts of his soldiers.

David achieved a great victory, rescued all his own, and his belongings, plus the spoil that Jehovah's enemies had. Because when we do what God says we will have his backing, and he will still give us more than we expect or ask for.

God expects us to seek him, to count on him, not to act foolishly. The greatest victories are achieved in intimacy with God.

Chapter 7: FUNDAMENTAL PRINCIPLES TO FACE AND OVERCOME THE CRISIS

Chapter 22 of the book of Genesis tells us one of the most difficult stages in the life of Abraham. Scripture says that "God tested Abraham" by asking what perhaps he loved most: his son Isaac.

But at the end of this story, Abraham is approved by God and manages to overcome this difficult moment in his life. Abraham witnesses a great divine intervention, we can observe several fundamental attitudes and actions to overcome adverse times and times of trial, actions that promote a miracle. Let's look at the principles for overcoming crises and start from this moment in Abraham's life:

Obey God by choice, not by emotion. Genesis 22:1-3.

Faced with a crisis, we can make big and serious mistakes by acting hastily, so it is essential to calm the heart and think calmly, observing the situation in detail to make the right decisions.

We see this when the text says that Abraham "got up early in the morning, got ready and went to the place that God told him". God had told him that he will travel to the land of Moriah and he did so, and when he saw the place from afar, he orders his servants to stay there and he continues the path with his son.

He did not question God, nor did he ask for explanations, he simply obeyed, and for this, he was blessed and honored by the Lord. It is very important to keep in mind that Moriah means "God provides" and also "vision", God teaches Abraham that he is the God who provides in every situation since he gave him the ram there to sacrifice instead of his son; and vision, reminding us that in all times, good or difficult, Jesus Christ must be our main vision "fixing our eyes on Jesus Christ".

Dialogue and support in others.

Abraham did not make this trip alone, he want with several of his servants. This reminds us of the importance of not fighting alone, of being accompanied by suitable and mature people in Christ, also seeking wise and prudent advice.

Let us therefore not dismiss dialogue as a component that helps us overcome the crisis, as an instrument of God to see things from other perspectives. The Bible also advises us to "pray for one another", this is spiritual support and strength to continue forward in the midst of difficulty.

The perseverance. Genesis 22:4.

Abraham could have fled (as Jonah fled to Tarshish when God sent him to Nineveh), or have renounced his faith in God (as Demas, of whom Paul says: "He has forsaken me, loving this world, and has gone to Thessalonica), or hiding like Adam (when he took its fruit from the forbidden tree), or playing the ignorant (like many of us), but Abraham persevered.

After traveling for three days (with his son and his servants), Abraham sees the place from afar and continues the journey, walking alone with his son, it was a difficult journey, through semi-desert land, now he begins to climb the mountain that God gave him.

He indicates, tired, with a more difficult path because he is climbing, thinking, and worrying about the future of his son, that of this family, remembering the promises of the Lord.

He had many things to overcome, but in spite of everything, Abraham kept going to the place that God had determined. Consistency demands a continuous rhythm, perseverance requires you to overcome obstacles.

Just as the clay supports the oil in the vessel, the character forged by the hand of God is the ideal container to carry the glory of the Lord.

The adoration. Genesis 22:5.

Abraham expresses his first objective to go there: "we will worship". The life of worship when it depends on the emotional state of the worshiper, is almost annihilated when difficulties come.

When the worshiper has learned that his God is the same in all circumstances and that he is God Almighty and good, he adores him above adversity, he adores him even though the path through which he travels is difficult and "incomprehensible".

Worship is focused on "who" God is, worship is focused on his person, which implies knowing him, worship is not born from intellectual knowledge, but from a personal relationship.

Abraham was not called a doctor of the law, nor a rabbi, nor a scholarly scribe, he was instead called: "friend of

God". Worship makes you walk the most difficult paths because you know who your God is.

Faith in God. Genesis 22:5.

Abraham says: "we will worship and we will return", confident that he will return with his son since God had told him: "through Isaac, your descendants will be prolonged".

What a great faith that of Abraham, what a way of speaking, what trust in God. Abraham as father is assuming a role similar to Heavenly Father when he dad to give up his Son.

The Holy Spirit reveals to us in the New Testament that Abraham obeyed God, thinking that he is powerful to raise even from the dead (Hebrews 11:17-19), so Abraham had all his trust in God (Today we have the record of resurrection miracles in Scripture and today, but at that time Abraham did not have them but believed).

Always walk trusting that God is aware of your situation, and he will take you to the place of your victory, God said to Abraham:

"Because you have done this, and you have not withheld your son from me, your only son; I will certainly bless you and multiply your descendants like the starts in the sky and like the sand that is on the shore of the sea, and your descendants will have victory over his enemies. In your seed, all the nations of the heart will be blessed".

What made Abraham stand out was precisely his faith in God. It is necessary to continue our journey of faith, without fainting or giving up; remember that true rest is only found in His presence, God is our strength, and he will not fail you.

Let us now consider the crisis the disciples went through when Jesus died on the cross and how they got through that time of crisis. Let's see then the principles that the Bible advises us here:

Strengthen your communion with God. John 21:1-3.

The disciples were not planning to evangelize or continue the ministry. As the Master is not with them, they experience a lack or direction. When we turn away from God, our hearts experience avoiding, and we easily undertake tasks or projects that are not part of God's plan for our lives.

By not counting on the direction of the Lord, energy and time are invested without results. This sea had several names: Sea of Galilee, Lake of Genesaret, and Sea of Tiberias, it was called a sea because of its large size compared to the country, but it really was a large freshwater lake.

It has been distinguished by its large number of fish. It is interesting that although the water was fresh and the fish were abundant, they were going through a sad moment, because "that night they did not catch anything". How difficult when one is dedicated to something and the result is zero.

Trust Jesus, he knows what to do and when to do it. John 21:4.

The Lord Jesus always comes at the right time. The Bible tells us: "When it was dawn" perhaps it was 5:00 or 6:00 in the morning, "Jesus appeared" surely the disciples returned discouraged.

The biblical text tells us that they "did not know it was Jesus" but here he manifested himself, so no matter how dark, difficult, and cold the night is our Sun of Righteousness will appear and shine, and the whole picture will change.

God's presence makes everything different (John 21:5-6). What a big difference between "all night they didn't catch anything" and "when they cast the net only once and they locked up a lot of fish". This teaches us that it is enough only to follow the Lord's direction.

When we follow God the results will be impressive. Miracles should bring us closer to Him. "That disciple whom Jesus loved" is John, who said to Peter: "He is the Lord". Peter got dressed, he did not want to presence himself without being covered before the Lord, this is how our encounter with Him will be, we must be covered with his justice and under his cover.

In this lake, the Lord Jesus performed 18 of the 33 recorded miracles. The Bible says that Peter: "jumped into the sea" because he wanted to get to see his Master first, he valued the presence of his Lord more than the blessings and miracles. He did not care about the fish, he wanted to be with his Master; he went beyond the miracle, he wanted the miracle worker.

In the face of discouragement, do not give up, renew yourself in God.

We cannot deny it, crises generate wear and tear, and depending on the duration of the crisis, they can generate resignation and abandonment. It is interesting to see that went the disciples return they return to shore Jesus has prepared all things (John 21:9-11).

The fish that the Lord was roasting was not one of the fish because of them. He always goes beyond what we think or expect.

The Bible tell us of "one hundred and fifty-three large fish" and "being so many the net did not break" in the original writing for "large" the Greek term "mega" is used, in this lake, there were 22 kinds of fish, some they reach one meter in length, we can of fish of 10 or 12 kilograms.

According to the context the disciples were seven (they all eat the same fish, it was therefore large) and therefore they now had a ton and a half of fish. We then see that Jesus transforms adverse circumstances into great victories.

Jesus knows your condition and cares for you (John 21:12-13). The Lord said to them: "come, eat" Jesus knew that they had been fishing all night and were hungry, He himself served them, although he was resurrected with all power, he took care of serving them (ministering to them).

Actually, the greatest miracle occurs when you meet Jesus (John 21:14). "Third time that Jesus appeared" the number three indicates divine fullness, perfection in witness. It is therefore a revelation of the Lord to his disciples, it is the risen Christ making himself known.

With the power of him Christ captivates your attention, with the love and care of him Christ captivates your heart, the love of God goes beyond a miracle. Do not give up, persevere God will act in your favor.

Some call the eleventh chapter of Hebrews the gallery of the heroes of faith, and a portion of this passage tells us: "By faith they conquered kingdoms, did justice, obtained promises, covered the mouths of lions", referring to Daniel, who by his faith in God was delivered from the lions.

Let's now consider a great example, the apostle Paul who had to face serious problems (Philippians 1:12-14).

Paul was in prison for serving the Lord and developing the ministry that God had entrusted to him. He was in prison in Rome at the time of writing this letter, he was not there for any personal crime.

Perhaps some brothers were discourage by this, but Paul argues that this has resulted in a blessing, he was evangelizing the Roman soldiers and the brothers outside inspired by Paul were preaching with greater passion.

The "problems" are opportunities where God wants to show the glory of him.

Let's try to get the right perspective. God wants to teach us in all the situations of our life; sometimes problems blind our vision, as we allow problems to afflict our hearts and it is difficult for us to see Almighty God.

In this case, Pablo's difficulty was jail, but it could be children, finances, marriage, leadership, etc. The apostle was strengthened in the joy of God, Philip. 4:4.

The joy of the believer should not be subject to circumstances but to God himself. Paul is encouraging the church from prison and tells them: "Rejoice in the Lord, always".

Regardless of the circumstances, your joys is in the Lord, and this makes you face your difficulties with height. Paul does not lament, nor does he feel sorry for himself, he strengths himself in God.

Paul did not admit or indulge resentment of problems, Philip. 4:5. The apostle instructs the church (the founding of the church in Philippi had many difficulties: persecuted, flogged, imprisoned… and in the Philippian jail Paul decided to worship God).

Difficulties that we do not submit to God upset us and we easily mistreat people, and we still allow bitterness in our hearts. Worship is a very powerful weapon to overcome problems because when we do it we look at the almighty God and by not concentrating on the problem, it makes it smaller.

The apostle Paul trusted God.

He decides to go to God and avoid heartbreak, Philip. 4:6. "Be anxious for nothing", other versions translate "anxious" as restless, afflicted, anguish, anxious, worried. The advice is to approach God and place the difficulty in his hands, giving thanks as an act of faith.

In Psalm 73 we see the psalmist with his mind confused and being tempted to do wrong, verses 12-16. But by entering the presence of God he managed to understand the character of God, verses 22-25, and he understood that although he sang and served in the temple, his heart had been moving away from God, that is, he had begun to doubt the power, goodness, and sovereignty of God, verses 27-28.

But in the end by the grace of God he understood what was happening. God knows us and knows what he does and allows.

The peace of God is a fortress against the enemy.

When you manage to place your circumstances in God's hands, true peace will come upon you, Philip. 4:7. Today's world seeks peace, and that is why drugs, medicines, tonics, nursing homes, but true peace is only found in Christ, and this peace surpasses our understanding because although the bars were before the eyes of Paul, he was joyful, calm and took advantage of the moment to evangelize the Roman prison.

We see then that Paul trusted God and went free; we see other examples when we trust God: The three young men trusted God and the fiery furnace could not harm them. Christ trusted in his heavenly Father and rose again.

We can trust in our God and we will win, we will see the glory of him because he said it: "everyone who believes in me will never be ashamed" that faith in God makes the peace of heaven flood the heart of the believer.

The peace of God is a shield that guards our mind, our intellect, we only find it by being in his presence, and when we allow God to do the work that we cannot do.

The ministry of Jesus faced many difficulties, just like the ministry of Paul, or of any of the men of God who impacted his generation, a life that transcends the normal will face difficulties.

It is necessary to be aware that we will have obstacles to overcome and that God will help us, not even the Son of God himself was example from this reality.

A Biblical Portion of the life of King David lets us see a great crisis caused by one of his sons: "And David went up the hill of Olives; and he climbed it crying, wearing his head covered and his feet bare.

Also, all the people that he had with him covered his head, and they were crying as they went up. When David arrived at the top of the mountain to worship God there, here is Hushai the Arkite who came out to meet him, his clothes torn, and land on his head", 2 Samuel 15:30-32.

Consider the circumstances of King David: his son Absalom wants to take away the throne. This is David's third son, he killed his brother Amnon (for he had raped his sister Tamar), and he prepared a plot against his father to become the king of Israel.

Absalom represents that family member or the close person who disappoints us or causes pain, and from whom such a thing would never be expected.

The battle David faces now is the greatest of his life. David faced Goliath, he lived the persecution of King Saul, and he faced many times the Philistine armies, many enemies, but he never planned to fight against his own son, he never expected that his own son would betray him.

It was not just another battle, it was a deeply personal and family crisis. Undoubtedly the biggest crises are those that occur in the bosom of our house, in this case, it is a son: Absalom (who rebels against his father).

Let us now consider King David's strategy in battle (v. 30). He climbs the olive trees (how interesting because it was the same thing that Jesus did before going to the cross).

He called the Mount of Olives because of their abundance there. He requires effort to climb. The olive tree symbolizes strength, shelter, and blessings.

The Mount of Olives was a favorite place for Jesus, where he taught his disciples (revelation), there he prayed (communion), and there he strengthened in prayer (renewal) to go to the cross.

Difficulties must lead us to victory. David was pushed by trouble onto this mountain. God knows what things we must face, God did not avoid the cross for Jesus, but he strengthened him to face it, and then he gave him a name above all names, he exalted him to the utmost.

Chapter 10: THE POWER OF THE WORSHIP OF GOD.

Worship is not only singing praises to God, this Word implies many things and its power raises the son of God above the difficulties and problems he faces. In addition, worship has impressive transforming power, since it leads the believer to the presence of God and there we are all transformed by his love and power.

We were chosen by the lord to be his children, and by his mercy and grace "we will be forever with the Lord", worshiping and serving him. Because of this truth, we should know much more about the privileges and blessings that we will have in heaven.

The Lord Jesus said: "In my Father´s house there are many mansions… I am therefore going to prepare a place for you", so let us prepare for the encounter whit the Lord Jesus Christ.

Jesus Christ is the foundation of our worship, and the presence of God requires a persevering longing from the worshiper. Revelation 1:9-11.

"I, John, who also am your brother, and companion in tribulation, and in the kingdom and patience of Jesus Christ, was in the isle that is called Patmos, for the word of God, and for the testimony of Jesus Christ. I was in the Spirit on the Lord's Day, and heard behind me a great voice, as of a trumpet, saying: I am the Alpha and the Omega, the first and the last, What thou seest, write in a book, and send it unto the seven churches which are in Asia…".

Ford the preaching of the gospel, the apostle John had been condemned and banished to an island called Patmos (this was a small island and was used as a penitentiary, where the Roman empire sent some prisoners, it was a desert and rocky island, there was no streams, no trees, the land was not fertile, except for some small plots).

In this place of adversity in worship in the Spirit, John listens to the Lord Jesus (Notice that John does not complain or murmur about his situation, what he is doing is persevering in worship despite everything). This teaches us that sometimes the Lord has deep and great teachings for us in the smallest and least beautiful places according to our opinion.

It is important to highlight here that the apostle John was in the Spirit, the Bible teaches us that: "Eye has not seen, nor ear heard, nor have they entered the heart of man, they are what God has prepared for those who love him. And he revealed them to us by the Holy Spirit", we see then that the relationship with the Holy Spirit is very important.

Our worship is inspired by the revelation we have of God.

It is interesting to take into account the name of this book: Apocalypse since this is its essence; apocalypse means: revelation, this name was given to it since it is the Greek term whit which the book begins (Revelation 1:1). This term is "apocalypse" which translates revelation or "unveiling" in the sense of running the veil (here we begin to see that worship generates open heavens).

The apostle John was worshiping the Lord, based on the revelation he had of God, but at that moment he would have new and powerful revelations of the Lord Jesus, of His church, and of His final and eternal plans:

The revelation of the Risen Jesus Christ, chapter 1.
The revelation of the condition of the seven churches of Asia chapters 2 and 3.
The revelation worship in heaven chapters 4 and 5.

The revelation of the coming judgments on our planet chapters 6 to 19.

The revelation of the last events and eternity chapters 20 to 22.

We can conclude that worship leads us to have a greater revelation of our God, let us remember that the Lord Jesus said: "This is eternal life: that they know you, the only true God and Jesus Christ, whom you have sent", it is because eternal life is a continuous and passionate knowledge of God, this requires a continuous and deep desire that must remain in our hearts.

The lexicon related to the worship service is very extensive in the word of God. But the essential concept is that of "service". The Hebrew and Greek terms both originally referred to the task of slaves or servants. Consequently, to offer this "worship" to God, his servants must prostrate themselves and thus manifest reverential fear and an attitude of admiration and respectful adoration.

On the way to the presence of God worship opens the heavens (Revelation 4:1)

"After this, I looked, and, behold, a door was opened in heaven: and the first voice which I heard was as it were of a trumpet talking with me; which said, Come up hither, and I will shew thee things which must be hereafter".

The heavens are opened on earth as a result of worship. The Bible tells us here: "Behold a door open in heaven", we can remember in light of this phrase the moment of Jesus's baptism: "and praying, heaven was opened, and the Holy Spirit descended on him", also in the times of the prophet Elijah the sky was closed for 3.5 years and there was no rain during that time, then the prophet prayed and the sky gave its rain; Let us also remember what the Bible says:

"Bring the tithes... and I will open the windows of heaven and pour out a blessing until it overflows", we can say then that worship sets the stage for the presence of God to manifest itself and when this happens anything can happen. Blessed be God who by His grace and power opened the heavens.

The Bible teaches us that one of the results of the open heavens is that the voice of God can be heard and the secrets and designs of heaven are received, we see for example that at the baptism of Jesus, the voice of the Heavenly Father was heard saying "This is my beloved Son".

Here in Revelation 4, the Bible tells. " the voice that I heard said" (whit the heavens open it is easier to hear God), the text adds "come up, I will show you the things that will happen" (the heavens open to reveal the condition present and plans of God).

The open heavens faciliate the revelation of the throne of God.

Revelation 4:2-3 "And immediately I was in the spirit, and, behold, a throne was set in heaven, and one sat on the throne. And he that sat was to look upon like a jasper and a sardine stone: and there was a rainbow round about the throne, in sight like unto an emerald".

Again the work and move of the Holy Spirit appear, says the bible text: "was in the Spirit", the Spirit of God leads us before the throne of the Lord and makes us more aware of the eternal truhs, the apostle Paul said:

The Bible teaches us that those who worship God must worship him in spirit and truth, and the Father seeks such as will worship him (John 4:24). Their delight is in what He is. Their joy is in God and they love him, glorying in him (Romans 5:11).

Worshiping God "in spirit" means worshiping according to the true nature of the Lord, and in the communion-giving power of the Holy Spirit. Because of this, it stands in contrast to worship consisting of religious forms and ceremonies, and to the religiosity of the flesh. To worship "in truth" means to worship the Lord according to the revelation that He has given in the grace of himself.

It is very interesting to see here that before the throne of God there is continuous worship, Revelation 4: 4, 6, and 8. Considering that the phone is synonymous with power and government, we can conclude that worship opens the heavens and allows the establishment of the government. Of God on earth, as well as promoting the flow of His power.

The Lamb of God receives continual worship in heaven.

Revelation 5:6-8 "And I beheld, and, lo, in the midst of the throne and of the four beasts, and in the midst of the elders, stood a Lamb as it had been slain, having seven horns and seven eyes, which are the seven Spirits of God sent forth into all the earth. And He came, and took the book from the right hand of him that sat on the throne.

And he came and took the book out of the right hand of him that sat upon the throne. And when he had taken the book, the four beasts and four and twenty elders fell down before the Lamb, having every one of them harps, and golden vials full odors, which are the prayers of the saints".

Christ is worthy of all worship. In this portion of the Scriptures we can see many important things, which are worth highlighting now:

1) Four living beings: they are angelic beings created by God that reflect the sovereignty and power of God.

2) Twenty-four elders: these represent the twelve tribes of Israel (old testament) and the twelve apostles of the Lamb (New Testament). They represent the fusion of the Old and New Testament, they reveal God in his different times and purposes, and they are like the representation of Israel and the Church.

3) A Lamb was slain: which reminds us of the glorious and complete sacrifice of Christ on the cross.

4) The number seven, the horns, the eyes, the seven spirits of God: let us remember that the number seven in the bible represents completeness; the horns are a figure of power and the eyes speak of his total knowledge

(omniscience and foreknowledge of God, this means that God knows everything just as he knows what will happen).

5) The book: the final judgments are written there (in heaven there are several books, among them, for example, the book of life).

6) Harps: they are instruments of worship, the scriptures also mention: trumpets and flutes in heaven.

7) The golden cups are divine containers, whit incense that was a priestly task to burn. The incense represents the players of the believers on earth (here we can see how much value the players of his children have for God since they are collected in these precious vessels).

Those redeemed by the blood of Jesus worship the Lord.

Revelation 5:9-10 "And they sang a new song, saying, Thou art worthy to take the book, and to open the seals thereof: for thou was slain and has redeemed us to God by thy blood out of every kindred, and tongue, and people, and nation; and hast made us unto our God kings and priests: and we shall reign on the earth".

The Bible tells us that they "sang a new song", this song is new because no other person has sung it and at no other time has it been done. It is a new song, and the bible teaches us that we should sing a new song to the Lord.

For example, Isaiah 42:10 says: "sing to the Lord a new song, his praise from the end of the earth", also in Psalms 33:3, 40:3, 96:1 "sing to the Lord a new song; sing to the Lord, all the earth", 98:1, 149:1 "sing to the Lord a new song, his praise be in the congregation of the saints".

God example us to raise a new song, regardless of our voice and ability to build a song, because it is the spirit who guides us, just do it for God in secret, whit simplicity and love for him.

In this passage we are given at least two reasons to worship the Lord Jesus Christ, the first: "with your blood, you have redeemed us", the expression "lamb" reminds us that in the old testament the sacrifice of an innocent animal was necessary and without defect so that the sinner could achieve forgiveness.

When john the Baptist sees Jesus coming to the Jordan for his baptism he said: "Behold the Lamb of God who takes away the sin of the world" revealing to us that the sacrifice of lambs in the OT was a symbol of the great sacrifice of Jesus for our sins.

The text of Revelation also tells us: "He has made us kings and priests for our God" that is, the Lord whit his sacrifice made us participants in his reign, in his presence, and in the highest privileges of being at his service (the bible teaches us that we will reign with him and that we will be forever whit the Lord).

The worship of our God has been described as "the honor and adoration that is rendered to Him because of what He is Himself and what He is to those who give it to Him"

The worshiper is supposed to be in a relationship with the Lord, and there is a prescribed order of service or worship. The people of Israel had been redeemed from Egipt by the mighty hand of God, and for this reason, as redeemed people, they could come to the place appointed by Him to worship following His instructrions.

God is looking for worshipers, with hearts passionate about His presence, with a deep desire to know Him, and the Bible teaches that He will respond by manifesting His glory, by seeking His face, and by persevering worship, the heavens are opened and the Holy Spirit will come upon you in a very special way, you will know the secrets and designs of God, and you will understand more fully the great price that the Lord Jesus paid for you.

Worship brings the presence and glory of God

We generally do things the way we like. When it comes to our spiritual life we must seek the guidance of the Lord, to do things as God pleases.

When we talk about our life of communion with the Lord, we must allow the Holy Spirit to guide and instruct us to it according to His will and purpose. So we must ask ourselves, how does God like me to worship him, or seek him? The greatest wealth that any man can have is the presence of God.

The sweet singer of Israel. 2 Samuel 23:1-2 "These are the last words of David. Said David son of Jesse, said that man who was lifted on high, the anointed of the God of Jacob the sweet psalmist of Israel says: The Spirit of the Lord has spoken by me and his word has been in my tongue.

King David was also noted for being a great worshipper

He was called "the sweet singer of Israel", his heart was after the heart of the Lord. From his adolescence taking care of the sheep of his father Jesse, David adored God with his songs and was a great prophet of the Lord.

We then observe the profound relationship between worship and the prophetic spirit, between the atmosphere of worship and the moving of the Spirit of God. In an environment of worship the power of the Lord moves, worship attracts the presence and manifestation of God.

David wrote many psalms and designed instruments of worship for the Lord. God himself expressed on several occasions how much he loved David, and placed him as king in the mids of his people.

One of the titles of the Lord Jesus is "son of David"; the name David means "beloved" or "beloved", and the Lord promised him that not one of his descendants would be missing from the throne of Israel. We must conclude that worship promotes and established the government and action of God in the midst of men.

King David was a worshipper, Psalm 146:1-2 "Hallelujah! O my soul, praise Jehovah. I will praise Jehovah in my life; I will sing psalms to my God as long as I live".

These last chapters of the book of psalms are written when David was old, and each one of them is an invitation to praise the Lord. Although David failed God, and its consequences were dire and painful, we see here a man with a heart that seeks the Divine presence. His virtue was to develop a heart whose desire was God himself.

Worship promotes real experiences with God. Psalm 51:10-12 "create in me a clean heart O God, and renew a right spirit within me. Do not cast me out from before you, and do not take your Holy Spirit from me. Restore to me the joy of your salvation, and the free spirit sustain me".

In the Book of Psalms, we see David experiencing various situations, we see him approach the Lord to give thanks, adore him, ask for his help, ask for forgiveness, etc. despite all his mistakes and sins, he had the virtue of submitting and humiliating himself before God and surrendering his heart to divine correction. King David was a person of great intimacy with God, and this is something we should emulate.

In that intimate communion, King David developed that prophetic spirit that God used to lead him in the construction of such beautiful and edifying psalms (lyrics inspired by the Holy Spirit that continue to edify and bless millions of people in the world and forever). Worship is a virtue of the born-again spirit that brings the presence of God.

The story of David and the Ark of the Covenant.

The Ark of the covenant represents the presence of the Lord. The ark was built when the Israelites built the tabernacle in the desert at the direction of the Lord, built of acacia wood and covered with gold, it represents the presence of God, and there God manifested his glory and spoke to Moses.

When the ark was brought to the battlefield, Israel was victorious over its enemy. But in the time of King David, the ark of the covenant was not in Israel, and David whose heart yearned for the presence of the Lord seeks to bring it (2 Samuel 6:12).

The ark was moved with great joy. 2 Samuel 6:12 "and it was told King David, saying, The Lord hath blessed the house of Obed-edom, and all that pertaineth unto him, because of the ark of God. So David went and brought up the ark of God from the house of Obed-edom into the city of David with gladness".

The Bible tells us that "David carried the ark of God with joy", other versions say: "rejoicing, merriment, jubilation, hubbub, with parties", and we see then that a worshiper experiences and lives the joy of God in his life.

They also did it with thanksgiving, 2 Samuel 6:13 "and it was so, that when they that bare the ark of Lord had gone six paces, he sacrificed oxen and fatlings".

A worshiper does not complain or murmur, because his eyes are not fixed on the problem but on the greatness of the One who receives his worship. Genuine worship is centered on the will and sovereignty of God which is why it considers that everything that comes from the Lord is good.

The glorious presence of the Lord produces expressive praise. 2 Samuel 6:14-15 "and David danced with all his might before the Lord, and David was clothed in a linen ephod. So David and all the house of Israel brought up the ark of the lord with jubilation and the sound of a trumpet".

The Bible tells us that on this occasion there is dance, praise with joy, and instruments, it was a special moment and that is why joy is expressed strongly and they resort to their instruments to glorify God.

King David was a worshipper, he was a man honored by the Lord. 2 Samuel 7:8-9 "Now therefore so shalt thou say unto my servant David, Thus saith the Lord of hosts, I took thee from the sheepcote, from following the sheep, to be ruler over my people, over Israel; And I was with thee whithersoever thou wentest, and have cut off all thine enemies out of thy sight, and have made thee a great name, like unto the name of the great men that are in the earth".

The Bible teaches us that God is looking for worshipers, perhaps anonymous people, as happened one day with David (taken from behind the sheep), but they are passionate hearts for God, who long to know him more, and whose joy is doing the will of God.

God honors those who honor him, magnifies God and He will give you places of blessing and privilege on earth, and always keep in mind: he is the most important, he is the reason for our life, all the glory belongs to him.

Israel's life in the Promised Land was also full of challenges of faith, the enemies and obstacles that appeared in the process of conquest and the temptation are Canaan demanded of the Hebrews fidelity and trust in God, things that the Lord also expects of us today.

Without a doubt, Abraham is an example of faith not only for Israel but for all believers today. By himself, we learn that faith in God will be rewarded.

God rewards those who seek him.

Hebrews 11:6 "But without faith, it is impossible to please him: for he that cometh to God must believe that he is and that he is a rewarder of them that diligently seek him".

The text tells us that faith, pleases God, and it is very interesting to see that in this verse faith is related to drawing near to the Lord. And he adds at the end "those who seek him" so he refers to those who persevere with faith in prayer and worship.

Of these, the verse says they will be "rewarded" that is, rewarded, rewarded by God Himself. Seeking the divine presence requires faith and perseverance and will never be in vain because the Lord will not only give an answer to the search but will reward those who do so with faith and perseverance.

God rewards those who trust in him. Hebrews 11:8 "By faith Abraham, being called, obeyed to go out the place which he was to receive as an inheritance; and he went out not knowing he was going".

When God calls Abraham his life was practically settled, however before the voice of God he obeys leaving his land, the Bible tells us without where he was going, he trusted God´s words.

The Lord promised Abraham blessings and inheritance, God told him: "I will make you a great nation, I will bless you, I will make your name great and you will be a blessing". And indeed the Lord blessed him, protected him in a supernatural way, and placed him in places of privilege and honor, even today he continues to be an inspiration for the church and is the father of all who is of the faith. God blesses those who trust in him.

Faith in God goes far beyond earthly security.

Hebrews 11:9-10 "By faith, he sojourned in the land of promise, as in a strange country, dwelling in tabernacles with Isaac and Jacob, the heirs with him of the same promise: for he looked for a city which hath foundations, whose builder and maker is God".

Abraham had to overcome various obstacles along the way, but God went with him and he finally reached the land where he wanted to take him. However, Abraham did not consider the Promised Land his own, he knew that God is the owner of everything

There are several things that we can see and highlight in the life of Abraham while he was in the land of Canaan. Security in eternal things determined his lifestyle on earth:

a) He knew that he was a stranger in the land. Our citizenship is heavenly. Here we are on the way.

b) He knew that the blessing and the promises would continue on his descendants (the role of our children in the divine plans is vital).

c) Abraham knew of the heavenly city. This is very interesting because today we have a greater revelation of that city according to the prophets, the epistles, and especially the book of Revelation, but he believed in that city in such a way that it transformed his earthly way of life.

When our hearts trust in God despite adversity, he does not leave his children in shame. The Lord manifests his power over those who trust in him and rewards those who seek him.

When the apostle Paul is shipwrecked on his trip to Rome, he manages to reach the island of malta and there he makes a campfire with the others who were saved, and a viper fleeing from the fire catches on his hand, and he shook it and suffered no harm. God protected him, it is interesting that the snake ran away from the fire. Fire speaks to us here of heat, light, and protection, among others.

Let us remember that Paul also said to Timothy: "kindle the fire of the gift of God that is in you". Fire is one of the symbols of the Holy Spirit, and that fire must be kept burning because his work is fundamental in our walk of faith.

Communion with God is of the highest value.

It is vital to recognize that God is good and is the source of your life. Gratitude generates adoration, Genesis 12:7 "And the Lord appeared unto Abram, and said, unto thy seed will I give this land: and there builded he an altar unto the LORD, who had appeared unto him"

God visited Abram and gave him a promise that involved a miracle since he still had no son, Sarah was barren and they were both elderly. Abram, grateful for God's promise, worships the Lord. The life of worship keeps the fire of God stoked in our hearts.

The altar tells us about death and produces life, Genesis 12:28 "Then he went from there to a mountain to the east of Bethel, and pitched his tent, having Bethel to the west and Hai to the east; and there he built an altar to the Lord, and called on the name of the Lord"

We know that generally, the altar was the place of sacrifice... it tells us about Christ, but also the place where God makes he will know to us, where the ego is sacrificed. And life because we receive from God his strength, his protection, and his direction... "He called on the name of the Lord..." on the previous altar (verse 7) there was gratitude, on this one (verse 8) there is dependence.

It is essential to diligently care for the fire of God in your heart, so persevere in the midst of difficulties, Genesis 12:10 "And there was a famine in the land, and Abram went down into Egypt to sojourn there; for the famine was grievous in the land".

He was in the Promise land, but the famine came and he went down to Egypt (sometimes even if we are in obedience to the Lord, trials will come)... God had placed him, but he did what most did descend to Egypt, looking for the "blessing" on the banks of the Nile River.

With the strengh of God, we can defeat selfishness and fears.

Genesis 12:11-13 "And it came to pass when he was come near to enter Egypt, that he said unto Sarai his wife, Behold now, I know that thou are a fair woman to look upon: Therefore it shall come to pass, when the Egyptians shall see thee, that they shall say, This is his wife: and they will kill me, but they will save thee alive. Say, I pray thee, thou art my sister: that it may be well with me for thy sake; and my soul shall because of thee".

Motivated by his ego and fear Abram plans his strategy; we must recognize that when there is fear of facing the uncertain, it is because we have neglected the altar of

God. The ego of our heart can lead us to put even our loved ones at risk. Communion with God generates benefits for all.

There is a powerful fuel for the fire of God, it is called obedience and we must not confuse it with cunning, Genesis 12:14-15

"And it came to pass, that, when Abram came into Egypt, the Egyptians beheld the woman that she was very fair. The princes also of Pharaoh saw her, and commend her before Pharaoh: and the woman was taken into Pharaoh´s house".

At first, the lie can bring a solution today, but it is pain for tomorrow, let us remember that the end does not justify the means. The Scripture says that "deceitful men will go from bad to worse", deceit and lies will never bring God´s blessing upon us.

At the moment of making decisions, he values God´s blessing more than the riches of Egypt, genesis 12:16-20

"And he entreated Abram well for her sake, and he had sheep, and oxen, and he asses, and menservants, and maidservants, and she asses, and camels. And the LORD plagued Pharaoh and his house with great plagues because of Sarai Abram's wife.

And Pharaoh called Abram, and said, What is this that thou hast done unto me? why didst thou not tell me that she was thy wife?

Why saidst thou, She is my sister? So I might have taken her to me to wife: now, therefore, behold thy wife, take her, and go thy way.

And Pharaoh commanded his men concerning him: and they sent him away, and his wife, and all that he had".

We can observe several very important conclusions:

1) Blessing is not always a sign of approval, look at the contrast in verses 16 and 17.

2) Abram did not build any altar in Egypt, but verses ago that was his characteristic.

3) Here she received the servant Hagar, a headache later on, for her home and for her offspring.

4) Abram left that land in shame.

We must take care of ourselves so that our first love for God remains valid and dynamic.

Restore and care for the altar (intimacy with God):

It is clear from Scripture that material abundance does not necessarily mean spiritual abundance, Genesis 13:1-2 "And Abram went up out of Egypt, he, and his wife, and all that he had, and Lot with him, into the south. And Abram was very rich in cattle, in silver, and gold."

Of course, God wants us to prosper, and that prosperity is integral, with the spiritual component being the priority. God wants us to govern the blessing, not for it to administer to us.

It is time to return to the altar, God awaits you, Genesis 13:3-4 "And he went on his journeys from the south even to Bethel, unto the place where his tent had been at the beginning, between Bethel and Hai, unto the place of the altar, which he had made there at the first: and there Abram called on the name of the Lord."

You can imagine that prayer, you can imagine that dialogue with God, and how much Abraham had to acknowledge. However, God´s plan with Abraham continues. Always keep in mind that God is faithful and will fulfill his purpose in us.

It is essential that our altar keep lit, and raise that "spiritual incense" pleasing to God. The altar of incense in the Old Testament tabernacle reminds us of that: a pleasing incense that was burned to God.

Some things appear in our lives and blow hard, trying to put out the fire of God in our hearts, and others spring from our hearts. But we do not have to wait for painful circumstances to recognize that we must take care of what God has deposited in our hearts.

Without a doubt, when the fire of God is lit in our hearts, faith in his power and care is strong. Faith is solid and is willing to obey and move forward in the face of the challenges that God puts before us. Every crisis becomes an opportunity to see the glory of God.

Although sometimes we think that God is taking a long time or that he has not listened to us, or that he has forgotten and perhaps the circumstances get worse, and others tell us that we cannot trust God. Everything is possible for him.

When making decisions we must take into account many things, and the most important thing in our case as children of God is to consider the law or advice of the Lord.

Let us remember that the "Cause and Effect Law" teaches us that everything we do will have a direct or indirect consequence, so the good future is determined by the good decisions of today. The correct conduct will always have good harvests. Abraham is an example of this.

The Lord Jesus paid a high price for our salvation, he renounced or stripped himself for a time of his heavenly glory, we can see his deep suffering and finally the delivery of his life in a horrible death, his spilled blood is what cleanses us from sin.

But it is the same Bible that teaches us that the Father honored him by exalting him to the highest. The life and ministry of the Lord Jesus were developed in complete obedience to the Father, it is to be considered that throughout his life the Lord Jesus maintained a powerful communion with God, since this is what strengthens us to do the divine will.

How to pray and seek the presence of God?

With a deep desire to please the Lord. Let's look at 2 Chronicles 34:1-2 "Josiah was eight years old when he began to reign, and he reigned in Jerusalem one and thirty years. And he did that which was right in the sight of the LORD, and walked in the ways of David his father, and declined neither to the right hand nor to the left".

We can consider several important things here:

a) Due to his age, it is most likely that Josiah was guided and instructed by other men of experience and wisdom from the royal court.

b) Neither his father Amon nor his grandfather Manasseh was noted for being godly or God-fearing men, 2 Chronicles 22:21-22. He did not repeat his story.

c) When the Bible tells us: "David his father" highlights his pious life, through which he imitated one of his ancestors, King David.

d) Keep in mind: "Your past does not have to determine your future." Although his father and grandfather were not god-fearing kings, Josiah was an excellent king, he reigned with God (and this made all the difference).

Seeking God must be a firm decision (2 Chronicles 34:3-4)

"For in the eight years of his reign, while he was yet young, he began to seek after the God of David his father; and in the twelve years he began to purge Judah and Jerusalem from the high places, and the groves, and the carved images, and the molten images.

And they brake down the altars of the Baalim in his presence; and the images, that were on high above them, he cut down; and the groves, and the carved images, and the molten images, he brakes in pieces, and made dust of them, and strowed it upon the graves of them that had sacrificed unto them".

We must highlight several important details here:

a) At the age of 8, Josiah begins his reign.

b) At the age of 16 (that is, "after 8 years of his reign") Josiah makes the decision to seek the Lord, and it is very interesting to see that as he got closer to God, he was able to identify that there were things to fix and others to improve.

c) At 20 years of age (years 12 of his reign) Josias begins a cleaning work, we speak of the images (idolatry) and cults whose practice implied the sacrifice of children, ritual prostitution, and the abundant and disorderly intake of wine, among others. It is very interesting to see here the close and logical relationship between seeking God and removing what the Lord does not like.

d) At 26 years of age (year 18 of his reign) Josiah begins the restoration or repair of the house (temple) of Jehovah.

e) The actions of king Josiah cut off those things that were making Judah sick and brought a time of restoration and revival to the people. Let us remember here that his name Josiah means "Jehovah heals", and this was what Judah received.

f) It is very important to have a defined daily time to seek God and a place to do it.
Basically praying is talking to God.

Sincere repentance is essential (2 Chronicles 34:18-19).

"Then Shaphan the scribe told the king, saying, Hilkiah the priest hath given me a book. And Shaphan read in it before the king. And it came to pass when the king had heard the words of the law, that he rent his clothes".

We must reflect on several expressions here:

a) The expression "he tore his clothes" is a phrase of pain before reading the Book of the Law found while they were repairing the temple (that is the power of the Word of God that converts us and transforms our lives).

b) With a sincere heart King Josiah sought to settle things with the Lord: 2 Chronicles 34:20-22. We see that it was not simply remorse, he made the decision to make profound changes in his life, Josias took measures that implied real changes in his normal life.

c) Hulda, the prophetess, wife of Salum, it is very interesting that her name Salum means "reward" and the Lord had rewarded him with a pious and God-fearing wife, she was a guardian of the court robes, she was recognized as a woman of God, and teaches the Jewish tradition that had a school in the city of Jerusalem.

d) The attitude of King Josiah´s heart (sincere, meek, and humble)pleased God and that is why he obtained the Lord´s blessing, verses: 26-28. To seek God we must divest ourselves of rituals and religious forms, to do it with simplicity and sincerity of heart.

Seeking God requires a deep yearning to live for him: 2 Kings 23:25.

"And like unto him was there no king before him, that turned to the Lord with all his heart, and with all his soul, and with all his might, according to all the law of Moses; neither after him arose there any like him".

This passage is a great challenge for us because it says that "there was no other king before him, who turned to the Lord with all his heart, with all his soul and with all his strength, according to all the law of Moses; nor was another like him born after him", we speak of a genuine, true and complete conversion.

His conversion to God was a very strong testimony because he not only preached with his words but with a lifestyle transformed by the power of the Lord. Praying and seeking God should be a lifestyle.

We must seek a sensitive heart for God. Just as the Bible highlights the conversion of king Josiah and the blessing and support to keep a heart sensitive to God all the time of our walk as children of God. On earth:

a) During the following 13 years God prospered him abundantly and in everything.

b) But at the age of 39 something sad happened in his life: 2 Chronicles 35:20-24.

c) Several revivals in the history of the church have lasted a short time, for example, the revival in Wales lasted 2 years, in Spain (several months), in Azusa USA (approximately 7 years), etc.

d) But for example Moses lived in love with God, sensitive to his voice, until the day of his death at 120 years of age.

e) Jacob died at the age of 147 (Gen. 47:28) adoring the Lord, Hebrews 11:21 "By faith Jacob when he died, blessed each one of the sons of Joseph, and worshiped leaning on the end of his drone. Let us ask God to give us a passionate heart for him every day of our lives.

Seeking God is a privilege that God himself gives us, that concern for him must be fed every day, and with his help, we can listen to his voice and do his will.

Jesus taught a lot about prayer.

In the face of difficulties or great obstacles we can think of doing many things, and we can even put prayer aside. That is precisely what the darkness seeks, but the Lord Jesus encourages us to pray and not lose heart. Everyone who asks will receive, God is not indifferent to your prayer.

The Lord Jesus regarding prayer taught in Matthew 7:7-8 "Ask, and it shall be given you; seek, and ye shall find;

knock, and it shall be opened unto you: For every one that asketh receiveth; and he that seeketh findeth, and to him that knocketh it shall be opened."

This with respect to constant prayer is motivated by faith in the power of God.

As we can see there are several verbs that invite us to action: ask, search, and call.
They are words that not only indicate doing something but also teach us that we must be an active part in generating God´s response.

We cannot be passive or indifferent when it comes to prayer, we have to engage in a diligent and persevering cry.

It is also very interesting to see that there are three main verbs here: ask, seek and find, because in the Bible the number three indicates perfection in testimony, that is, this confident and persevering prayer stands as a powerful testimony before God whose strength touches the heart. Heart of the Lord who will not be still or silent.

It is a prayer in which not only one speaks with God, it is one that presents with a request the deep yearnings of the heart that with simplicity but with faith are presented before the Sovereign God, Lord, and owner of fall things. It is a cry that recognizes that the power and highest authority is God Himself.

The Lord Jesus teaches us that constant and trusting prayer reaches powerful answers from God, the person who prays and perseveres tells us the biblical text: "he will receive, he will find and it will be opened".

Then the blessings and answers will come to the one who prays, the closed doors will be opened for the one who cries out. No person who cries out to God will come away empty-handed.

The Lord Jesus teaches us according to Matthew 7:9-11

"Or what man is there of you, whom if his son asks bread, will he give him a stone? Or if he asks for a fish, will he give him a serpent? If ye then, being evil, know how to give good gifts unto your children, how much more shall your Father which is in heaven give good things to them that ask him?

A very important factor is added here in the faith of the one who prays, and it is the goodness of our heavenly Father.

If earthly parents with a sinful or fallen nature try to give good things to their children when they ask, much greater and more perfect is the goodness of God the Father who will respond with the best of heaven to the cry of his children. It is then fundamental to believe in the goodness of God and his fidelity and power.

The biblical text tells us that God "will give good things to those who ask" a phrase that teaches us that God´s goal is to bless with "good things" and these things are not necessarily what we want, but those "good" according to the purpose and nature of our heavenly Father.

These things will be for those who "ask" as Jesus tells us. Therefore, the requirement here is to ask, a matter that undoubtedly implies faith in the first instance. Well, if we don´t believe, we wouldn´t even take the initiative to pray.

This portion ends with what is known as the Golden Rule: "whatever you want men to do to you, do so them." We see here once again the principle of sowing and reaping, then every injustice that man sows will be the injustice that he will reap.

The good, rectitude, and goodness that we hope that men have with us are precisely the good, rectitude, and goodness that we must sow today.

Just as in the natural, sowing implies effort and overcoming obstacles, and the harvest gives us his strength and help, he will not only listen to us but will respond with kindness and love, and he will not be indifferent to the cry of his children.

Search knock and ask, because God will answer you by allowing himself to be found, he will bless you and open doors for you that only his power can open.

No matter the situation in which we find ourselves, our hearts must always be willing to seek God, because he is our help and help. Let´s look at the case of the prophet Jonah, who invoked God from his anguish.

"Then Jonah prayed to the LORD his God out of the fish's belly, and said, I cried by reason of mine affliction unto the Lord, and he heard me; out of the belly of hell cried I, and thou heardest my voice" Jonah 2:1-2.

As we read the story of Jonah, we see that he had listened to God, and had fled from him in a ship, had slept there, and had even talked with the sailors, but only now do we see that he prays ("Then Jonah prayed").

Of course, I didn't pray before because I was running from God. Sometimes the believer does not pray. He is fleeing from God because he knows that the Lord will remind him of His will.

We can pray in the kitchen, on the street, in the car, and even in the bathroom, but no one would plan to pray in the belly of a big fish. For a moment, let's try to imagine it… But this was the scenario that Jonah chose when he disobeyed God.

The Lord's prophet had made his way to Tarshish, and this did not take God by surprise because "the Lord had prepared a great fish to swallow Jonah." Many times

we, having had the opportunity to pray in a beautiful and comfortable setting, end up praying out of crisis or pain.

How many thanks we must give to God who gives us life to invoke His name, our heart rejoices when amid praise in the temple we invoke His name.

But in this case, Jonah invokes God amid anguish: "I invoked Jehovah in my anguish", the term anguish here comes from the Hebrew: "tsarah" which also translates: to affliction, trouble, tribulation, and this condition took Jonah to pray.

The truth is that a good number of times, we only turn to prayer when the anguish, crisis, or difficulty hits home.

But how beautiful is the phrase: "and he heard me", that is the hope that should feed our faith, knowing that in the temple, in the street, in the kitchen, going or fleeing, we can raise our sincere, simple prayer, from a heart that raises its eyes to heaven and turns to God, and will be heard by the Lord.

It is not because of our merits, it is because of His great mercy and grace towards His children. God's response is not in vain, His mercy is manifested to His purpose: to teach Jonah and save the Ninevites.

As children of God, we have the privilege of speaking with our heavenly Father, and he also wants to not only speak to us but that we obey him.

Sometimes we must invoke God out of anguish, as a consequence of our bad decisions, but if we do it with a heart that turns to Him, God hears us and responds, organizing everything according to his will and goodness.

Prayer is a powerful weapon for spiritual battle.

God himself throughout his word teaches us the immense power that prayer has, thus becoming a powerful weapon of spiritual warfare. For example, Israel had enemies to face through the desert while walking to the Promised Land and prayer was a powerful weapon for the battle.

At a certain moment, Amalek rose against Israel, the Hebrews must face a great army, and Moses commissions Joshua to lead the Israelite army (we must bear in mind that several of the battles are fought by the Lord directly in our favor, but others we must face us, of course with His power and help and when doing so the victory is ours).

Exodus 17:10-11 tells us that "So Joshua did as Moses had said to him, and fought with Amalek: And Moses, Aaron, and Hur went up to the top of the hill. And it came to pass when Moses held up his hand, Israel prevailed; and when he let down his hand, Amalek prevailed".

Let us try to see adversities rather as opportunities in which the Lord will manifest his power and glory, this helps us grow as soldiers of his army.

The Hebrew people had to prepare for battle since Canaan would require them to face many battles, so this was an opportunity planned by the Lord to form and train his people since there were many things ahead of them.

It is very important to keep in mind that Deuteronomy 25:17-18 tells us that Amalek attacked Israel from behind, textually telling us that: "the rearguard of the weak defeated you… when you were tired and worked".

We see that which Amalek hunting lion, as well as the enemy of the Christian, seeks to attack the weak and those who are tired, that is why the believer must constantly renew his strength in God through prayer and "watching for it with all perseverance", in the Lord is strong, he is our hiding place, castle, and strong rock.

The Bible teaches us that Joshuah with his army went down to the valley to fight Amalek, while Moses went up to the top of the mountain to pray from there. How important to see here that each one, according to what he has received from God, exercises the gifts delegated by the Lord for the benefit of the people.

Joshua represents the man of battle and action, while Moses represents the man of revelation and prayer, and both are vital and in turn represent the balance that the

Lord expects from his soldiers: prayer and action. So it must be.

The fact that Moses is at the top and Joshua struggles in the valley, teaches us the divine order: first the spiritual, first God, and then the natural, the material.

The Lord wants to direct the battles and conquests on earth, but it often happens that we start many things with our own strength, without God´s direction, because of this we see painful failures and great losses.

The Bible teaches us that when Moses´ hands were up, the army of Israel prevailed, and when he lowered them the opposite happened.

Surely our hands have been tired on many occasions, as human beings it is natural that sometimes tiredness appears, but the reaction should not be to give up, or abandon dreams, but rather to lean on God and in supportive prayer, it was what Moses did, Aaron and Hur helped each other, and they held each other´s hands until they achieved victory over the enemy army.

Without a doubt, we face battles and some are more intense than others, but the Lord is the same and in him "we are more than conquerors", we are children of God with the authority and anointing to win. Do not give up your prayer, persevere, victory is near, and God is coming for you.

Chapter 13: HOW TO OVERCOME FEAR IN LIGHT OF THE BIBLE.

When the disciples were crossing the Sea of Galilee, a great storm arose and they thought they were going to die, so much so that they woke up Jesus and told him: "Don´t you care, we perish", he replies: "Why are you afraid?" Fear is an obstacle to overcome on our way to the destiny that God has prepared.

Fear is the antithesis of faith, since faith is the certainty of what God will do and the conviction of His presence, while fear is the certainty of misfortune to come and the conviction that God is not there.

That is why the kingdom of darkness tries to feed fear, but God has given us His word to strengthen faith, His victory on the cross to move forward, and His Holy Spirit to be brave.

In the first place, we must make a difference between the fear of God and fear.

Definition of the word "fear" in the Bible. From the Hebrew "Yira" is a feeling of respect or reverence. This feeling comes from God. It refers to the ability to revere Him, that is, it empowers us to obey His commandments, avoid evil and maintain gratitude and recognition of all His favors.

The fear of God leads us to give the first place to his Word. We must value the fear of God in our hearts because the prophet Isaiah (33:6) says: "the fear of the Lord is his treasure." The fear of God leads us to turn away from evil.

The fear of God is the beginning of wisdom, Proverbs 1:7 "The fear of the Lord is the beginning of knowledge: but fools despise wisdom and instruction". The fear of God is the framework where holiness is strengthened and love for the purity of God grows: 2 Corinthians 7:1.

Fear according to the Bible:

Let's read for example Matthew 14:30 " But when he saw the wind boisterous, he was afraid; and beginning to sink, he cried out, saying: Lord, save me!"

The definition of this fear is translated from the Greek term "Fobeo" which also means: tremble, fear, be afraid.

The unpleasant and unpleasant sensation is caused by a sense of danger, or repulsion toward certain people or situations without an apparent justification. It is a feeling that causes flight.

The origin of fear is diverse, for example:

1) It is the first feeling that a man expresses after the fall ("I heard your voice, I was afraid and I hid").
2) Fears born in childhood (traumas).
3) Past and painful failures.
4) Fears instilled (those that other people projected on us).
5) By feelings of self-condemnation.
6) For unresolved sins.
7) For real or imagined threats.
8) The Greek term for fear is "fobeo", derived from the Greek root "Phobos". Which in turn gives rise to the word phobia.

Phobias are emotional health disorders that are characterized by a disproportionate fear of specific objects or situations. For example, claustrophobia (intense fear of closed places) or entomophobia (fear of insects), etc.

In Greek mythology, Phobos was the god of fear and panic. He appeared before each battle to instill fear and put the opposing army to flight. Bold and strong, he put to flight the most resistant fighter. His eyes of fire, his mouth full of teeth in a fearsome white row, and discord on his hard forehead caused the stampede of men.

It is interesting to see that its objective is to put to flight, to make the army or the warrior not even fight but become discouraged, fearful, and flee. Is it not also the goal of the kingdom of darkness?

The Bible tells us about the "spirit of cowardice" (fear, timidity):

2 Timothy 1:7 "For God hath not given us the spirit of fear, but of power and love, and of a sound mind".

The spirit that God has given us is one of power, love, and self-control. To win, to move forward, to conquer what God has destined for our lives. God has equipped us to walk in victory: Romans 8:15 and 1 John 4:18-19.

Fear stagnates, stops, and prevents the advance and conquest, Proverbs 29:25 "The fear of man bringeth a snare, but whoso putteth his trust in the Lord shall be safe".

Let us remember that Gideon was full of fear when God called him; Moses´ fears prevented him from accepting the Lord´s call in the first place. God over and over again tells his children, his servants: "Do not be afraid." Because fear is like a chain, a bond, that doesn´t let you move forward. Let us remember that "for this, the Son of God appeared to undo the works of the devil".

Don´t let fear run your life.

Faith in God leads us to walk safely and confidently, we believe that we can conquer the challenges that God puts before us. In contrast, fear prevents progress, fear stops, stagnates, and produces losses. We must believe in the power, sovereignty, and goodness of our God.

Fear affects the spiritual life. Let´s read Genesis 32:9-12 "And Jacob said, O God of my father Abraham, and God of my father Isaac, the Lord which saidst unto me, Return unto the country, and to thy kindred, and I will deal well with thee… deliver me, I pray thee, from the hand of my brother, from the hand of Esau: for I fear him… And thou saidst, I will surely do thee good, and make thy seed as the sand of the sea, which cannot be numbered for multitude."

Jacob is going through a time of anguish and fear, so he decides to pray, here it is very interesting to observe in detail the prayer he prays because we see that although he cites the promises of God, he does so with fear because he does not know how his brother Esau will react to the seeing him, he thinks that his brother is coming to kill him and not only him but his whole family.

He also prays that he is there because God himself sent him, but the crisis of faith led him to separate the people and their cattle so that they would not all die, fear affects our faith, and that is why it is important to pray, meditate and declare the promises of the Lord over our lives because faith is nourished by the word of God.

It is also very interesting to see that at the end of this chapter 32 Jacob has an encounter with the angel of the Lord, who is God Himself, his name is changed and he leaves there ministered by the Lord. So we see that amid Jacob's fear and anguish, God came to strengthen and transform him. So we see that God never forsakes us.

Fear affects our family.

Genesis 33:1-3 "And Jacob lifted up his eyes, and looked, and behold, Esau came and with him four hundred men. And he divided the children unto Leah, and unto Rachel, and unto the two handmaids. And he put the handmaids and their children foremost… And he passed over before them, and bowed himself to the ground seven times until he came near to his brother".

Jacob plans to appease his brother Esau´s anger and sends before him several herds of cattle: sheep, goats, camels, cows, donkeys, etc, and each herd was led by a servant of Jacob who had to deliver this gift to his brother (there was more than five hundred head of cattle).

Seeing his brother Esau, Jacob rushes and distributes his family, we see a man doing many things full of fear and anguish, and his family had to go through all this too. How many times out of fear do we not assume our responsibilities and that is around us suffer the consequences?

God does not give his strength to face and overcome the fear of speaking or dialogue, of making decisions, the fear of commitment or the fear of facing challenges in God makes the family suffer. Jacob struggled for years with a fear of the past, he believed that his brother Esau only thought of taking revenge.

In these situations, it is necessary to approach Jesus and allow his power to heal our hearts and bring freedom to our lives. God wants the best for us and for our family.

Finally, Jacob meets Esau who hugs him and together they cry. He has a wonderful encounter, then fear made Jacob believe things that weren´t true.

Fear affects our lifestyle.

When the giant Goliath challenged the army of Israel to send a warrior to meet him, everyone from King Saul was afraid. This fear did not let them advance and prevented them from seeing victory. David faced the giant because he was sure of God´s power and he won.

Fear is an obstacle that drives back kings and entire armies. But faith in the Lord achieves great feats.

Let´s read Judges 6:11 "And there came an Angel of the Lord and sat under an oak which was in Ophrah, that pertained unto Joash the Abiezrite: and his son Gideon threshed wheat by the winepress, to hide it from the Midianites."

The Bible teaches us that the angel of Jehovah is God himself (this is a theophany or visible manifestation of

God), in this case, he comes to call Gideon to raise him as the new liberator of Israel. In this dialogue, we can see the fears in the heart of the human being before a challenge, mission, or divine call.

We must take into account the historical moment of this biblical passage. The people of Israel had come out of slavery in Egipt, and had set in the Promised Land (Canaan), Moses, Joshua, and the elders of that time had already died.

The Lord had raised other leaders or judges in Israel such as Othniel, Ehud, and Deborah, among others. But the people of Israel had done evil, and for that reason, the Midianite oppression had come. Sin generates great losses (spiritual, emotional, and material): Judges 6:8-10.

Origin of that fear:

The Lord before the cry of his children comes to bring freedom and the chosen person is Gedeon, but he is captive in his fears or fears (the Bible tells us that: "Gideon threshed wheat by the winepress, to hide it from the Midianites" Judges 6:11).

Why is the human heart sometimes governed by fear? Let us now consider some factors that lead to fear and the influence of past traumatic experiences:

a) The influence of spirits of fear, Judges 6:10. The Bible also implicitly teaches us that there are spirits of cowardice, let's see: "God hath not given us a spirit of fear" 2 Timothy 1:7.

b) The failures of the past (past failures can stop future progress, precisely because of the fear of failing again).

c) Rejection (Continuous rejection in childhood can lead people to not try to achieve great goals so as not to receive more rejection. Rejection can also cause behaviors that are alien to the real person, just so as not to face more contempt).

d) Feelings of condemnation (the people of Israel had sinned and the Lord had delivered them into the hands of the Midianites for seven years, by that time the time of judgment had been fulfilled, but Israel was still captive in their fears).

e) The words of curse or contempt of people with authority over us that sealed the heart (for example parents, bosses, educational authorities, uncle, among others).

Fear profoundly affects lifestyle.

Fear is a tie or bond that paralyzes, stagnates, and influences a person´s lifestyle, the Holy Scriptures teach us: "The fear of man bringeth a snare: but whoso putteth his trust in the Lord shall be safe" Proverbs 29-25.

Let´s keep in mind that "Fear is to the kingdom of darkness, what faith is to God." Since faith is the certainty of what is hoped for, fear is the certainty of failure or fall; faith is the conviction of victory that is not seen; while fear is the conviction that everything is going to go very wrong.

That is why, faced with certain challenges in life, the person decides not to move forward, because according to her, everything will go wrong. So we see that fear determines lifestyle (just as faith does too).

The Bible tells us: "And the hand of Midian prevailed against Israel. And the children of Israel... caves were made in the mountains, caverns and fortified places" Judges 6:2 (from the Hebrew "Fortified place" translates: a natural place of difficult access, they fled seeking refuge and security, because of fear they changed the valley through mountains and caves).

Israel lived in fear, in scarcity, in great discomfort, in the midst of darkness and cold (the Bible tells us in verse 11):

Gideon was beating the wheat in the winepress.

The winepress was a suitable place to crush the grapes and obtain their juice, also to crush the olives and thus obtain the olive oil, it was not to shake the wheat, so why

did Gideon do it there? Surely it was a small amount and he was hiding, so we see that fear had affected his way of life).

Choose to believe in God and fear will fall (Hebrews 11:33-34).

It must be faith that drives us and determines our lifestyle. It is that faith that achieves great conquests and victories for God. Fear, in contrast, prevents us from moving forward and developing the Lord´s plan for our lives.

Fear is the weapon of darkness that seeks to prevent the advancement of the children of God.

Gideon decided to move forward, he decided to believe in God and the Lord ended up supporting him mightily and he became a hero of faith: Hebrews 11:29-32. Brave advances despite their fears and failures.

In the face of fear, we must go to the presence of God in prayer, declare his powerful words over our lives, and trust in his care and power, in this way we will leave our place of prayer strengthened in his power and with the faith to move forward.

Although sometimes it is hard for us to believe it, God is above all difficulties and adverse circumstances. No problem is greater than the power of the Lord.

Sermon one: God is bigger than your problem.

"When Joseph came to his brothers, they took away the colored tunic that he had on, and they threw him into the cistern, but the cistern was empty, without water… and when the Midianite merchants passed by, they took Joseph out and sold him… Joseph was taken into Egypt" Genesis 37:13-24,28.

Sometimes we do not understand the betrayal of the one who "loved" us. The story of the life of Joseph, son of Jacob, has a very high teaching content for us.

In this chapter, his brothers plan to kill him, but finally, they sell him as a slave, after having stripped him of his valuable colored tunic (note that unhealed resentment can become stronger than family love; they were his brothers and planned to kill him. The same thing happened to Jesus).

God never forsakes his children.

The biblical text tells us that Joseph is thrown by his brothers into a cistern (a cistern is an underground reservoir to store the water that gathered when it rained, or from springs), the text tells us literally: "but the cistern was empty", how significant is this "but", because we see the hand of God protecting his purpose.

It was not a coincidence that he was without water, it was part of the divine plan, and José would be in the cistern (but without water) for a short time. Let us remember that it is written: "My foot will not give way to the slide, nor will he who guards me sleep."

After spending some time in that cistern, some Midianite merchants appear and Joseph is sold by his brothers for twenty pieces of silver and his heart is deeply hurt; definitely, the most painful wounds are those caused by our intimates, those from whom a betrayal would never be expected.

Let us remember that Jesus was sold by one of his disciples, Judas Iscariot, that is why we can go to him, because he understands us perfectly and with his help we can emerge triumphant, raising the flag of forgiveness.

God acts in various ways.

These Ishmaelites "carried Joseph into Egypt" During all these circumstances was the hand of God, although Joseph was sold as a slave, he would be in the house of an Egyptian general, managing his state with the favor and supernatural grace of God.

Joseph was equipped and trained to be the second in the Egyptian empire and to be an instrument of blessing and salvation for thousands and thousands of people, including his father and the brothers who had one day rejected and betrayed him.

The purposes of the Lord are designed for the salvation and blessing of many, that is why the darkness is opposed, but the purpose of God prevails, the Lord strengthens, guards and protects his children to lead them to victory.

Sermon two: God wants to act on your behalf.

Separated from God we can do nothing. Nothing is transcendent, nothing that is useful in the kingdom, nothing that impacts the glory of God. When we do things that God is not, it is like plowing metal, watering seed on dry land, or blowing the wind, we will not have positive results.

But, when we decide to follow the will of God, walk in His times and submit to His will, we will see giants fall (like Goliath), great obstacles are removed (like the walls of Jericho) and great doors will open (like the Red Sea). For the sons of God to pass.

Genesis 39:2-5 "But the Lord was with Joseph, and he became a prosperous man... So Joseph found favor in the eyes of the Egyptian and served him, and he made him steward of his house and gave all that he had into his power, and from when he gave him charge of his house, Jehovah blessed the house of the Egyptian for Joseph's sake".

The most important thing is that God is with you.

Today's biblical text highlights the Lord's supernatural blessing on Joseph in the house of Potiphar, the Egyptian captain, and the reason is stated in the first sentence: "But the Lord was with Joseph".

How interesting, his brothers had rejected him, his father believe he was dead, and Joseph was in a foreign land (in Egypt) but he was not alone, God was with him, and this is the most important thing.

The Bible also teaches us: "and he was a prosperous man", the Hebrew term for "prosperous" used here is "tsalákj" which also translates: push forward, succeed, achieve (which allows us to see the attitude of faith, thriving and Diligence of José, despite the adverse circumstances).

When we obey God His favor accompanies us.

Joseph found favor in the eyes of Potiphar, that is, the favor of the Lord was with Joseph. The favor of God is that virtue, it is that superior spirit, it is that radiance, granted by the Lord that makes his children stand out, that supernaturally supports the trades, professions, or projects entrusted or delegated to the children of the Lord.

Let us remember what the Scripture says of the prophet Daniel: "Daniel himself was superior to these satraps and governors because a superior spirit was in him, and the king thought to set him over the whole kingdom" Daniel 6:3.

Integrity and the fear of God walk together.

Captain Potiphar gave Joseph everything he had made him steward of his entire house. God was using the Egyptians with all his heritage, to form the future ruler of the Egyptian empire (Joseph was about 20 years old).

Joseph not only administered the Lord's grace well with him, but the fear of God is
Evident in his heart (the fear of God is that treasure or blessing that leads us to turn away from the path of evil, to walk the path of integrity).

Although Joseph had great autonomy over Potiphar's assets, he was honest and upright. He did not have the Bible like we do today, nor did he live the fullness of the Holy Spirit (New Testament experience) and he was in a foreign land, he did not give in to the offers of Potiphar's wife, nor to her pressures, on the contrary, he said:

"My lord has put in my hand all that he has... how then should I do this great evil, and sin against God?" (Without a doubt, it is an example to follow).

When God is with you, it will be evident to others.

Finally, the Scripture tells us "The Lord blessed the house of the Egyptian because of Joseph" and Potiphar was a witness. Joseph did not have to say it, nor did he announce it, the other saw it, and God Himself gave evidence of it (We do not have to shout to others that God is with us, he will simply bear witness to His presence).

That is why seeking the presence of God in our lives should be our priority. Strengthening and growing in our intimacy with God is fundamental, and the Lord himself wants to help us in this, that is why he sent his Son, his Holy Spirit, and his blessed Word.

Sermon three: God keeps us during the crisis.

Introduction: In the face of crises there are different reactions. For example, Israel wanted to return to Egypt through the desert, Jonah fled to Tarshish, Elijah, faced with Jezebel´s persecution, asked God to take his life, and when the Roman soldiers captured Jesus, the disciples fled.

These are the natural reactions to crises, but let us remember that Jesus persevered in prayer before the cross, and "an angel from heaven appeared to strengthen him". When the crisis is great, a greater power comes from heaven for you to overcome it.

Let us consider a moment in the life of Joseph, the son of Jacob when he was imprisoned in the prison of Pharaoh´s prisoners: Genesis 40:23 and 41:1,9, 14

"And the chief cupbearer did not remember Joseph but forgot him. It happened that after two years Pharaoh had a dream… Then the chief cupbearer spoke to Pharaoh… and Pharaoh sent and called Joseph. And they hired him out of prison, and he shaved, and changed his clothes, and came to Pharaoh.

Disappointments are part of the journey.

The Bible teaches us a new disappointment that Joseph experienced. Being in an Egyptian prison (and by the favor of the Lord he attended to all things in that place), he was assigned to serve the chief cupbearer and the chief baker that Pharaoh had sent there, and while there he interpreted their dreams for them, which were fully complied with.

Joseph then asked the chief cupbearer to remember him and speak to Pharaoh, but Pharaoh forgot. Surely it has also happened to us, that have served and blessed others, they quickly forget the favors received.

Let's walk in God's times.

The Scripture teaches us that "after two years Pharaoh had a dream". The phrase "after two years" tells us about time, sometimes time seems very long, but walking in God's times is something we must learn.

The divine intervention was not after six months, nor after five years, Pharaoh would have the dream two years after the cupbearer was released from prison. So, in reality, the cupbearer's forgetfulness was part of the divine schedule.

It is at this time (Joseph was 30 years old, Genesis 41:46) when the chief cupbearer spoke of Joseph to Pharaoh, and we see how God uses various means, resources, and people to finally bring us to His will (the Lord used to Potiphar, to the chief of the prison, to the chief cupbearer, and then to Pharaoh himself). Everything is possible for God.

Crises are stages of growth.

We see that Joseph was quickly brought out of jail to be brought before the Egyptian king. Being in jail and also without a just reason, is a crisis that several servants of the Lord experience, however, God always gave them the victory, and always showed His power in favor of their children.

It is good to remember how they faced prison: Joseph with integrity and diligence, Paul and Silas with adoration and praise, Peter and the early church with much prayer and intercession, and all of them witnessed the power of the Lord freeing them from their captivity. Therefore: The manifestation of the supernatural power of our God will always exceed the size of our difficulty!

God is more interested in your being than in your work.

Now Joseph must go to Pharaoh to interpret his dreams. God wants to use us in a great way, however, he wants to work first on our being (character) and then on our work (service).

In Joseph we see the manifestation of divine gifts, from his adolescence, he was seventeen years old when he was sold by his brothers and spent thirteen years between Potiphar's house and prison, places where he learned not only administration, but forgiveness, tolerance, humility, subjection, responsibility, etc, and further developed the gift received from heaven.

Now the Lord approves of his appearance in public, and Joseph is clear about his place because he says to Pharaoh."When our heart matures in the hands of God, it becomes an optimal container for the glory of the Lord. Persevere, God keeps us during the crisis.

Our whole life is in the hands of God, they are hands that protect us, hands that provide, and lead us to the divine purpose, and hands that form us, like the hands of the potter. For this reason, he advances in following Jesus, he knows what he is doing.

Sermon four: God is almighty to fulfill his plan for you.

Jacob left his son Joseph for dead, and his brothers sold him as a slave to the Midianites and brought his colored tunic stained with blood to his father, telling him that a beast had devoured him.

José remained imprisoned in the jail of the prisoners of the king for several years so that for his family he no longer existed. However, the Lord had a wonderful plan for him and when the time came he got him out of jail to make him the second ruler in Egypt after Pharaoh, and from there save multitudes, including his own family:

Genesis 45:7-8 "And God sent me before you, to preserve your offspring on the earth, and give you life by a great deliverance. Therefore it was not you who sent me here, but God, who has made me the father of Pharaoh, and lord of all his house, and ruler over all the land of Egypt."

That's why keep In mind: You are God's plan, he will strengthen you to overcome difficulties because many sinners, sick, and captive await you, they need the message of God that you have, persevere the Lord wants to use you powerfully.

Despite all the obstacles, sorrows, and disappointments that José had to live with, God was aware of every step, the Lord was acting in the midst of all that because he was leading José to the destiny that he had prepared for him.

Sometimes we live in situations that are very difficult to understand, but the most important thing is that our life is in the hands of God, and he will do what is best. His power and goodness are above all the obstacles and powers of the enemy.

On many occasions, it is difficult for us to fully understand the work of God, but what the Bible teaches us is to trust in him, the Lord is good and knows very well what he does and when he does it. Persevere, trusting in God, he will take you to your best destination.

We hope that this book has been to your liking.

We invite you to know all the books that the author has published: Pastor Gonzalo Sanabria

www.ingramcontent.com/pod-product-compliance
Lightning Source LLC
Chambersburg PA
CBHW052103150726
48002CB00006B/2197